DAVID GATWARD

Everyday

prayers

about

early

mornings,

MONDAY MORNINGS
AND TRAFFIC JAMS

coffee

breaks

and

weekends

that

go

too

quickly

kevin
mayhew

*For anyone who's realised that work is
just what's happening in their life,
rather than why their life is happening.*

First published in 2003 by
KEVIN MAYHEW LTD
Buxhall, Stowmarket
Suffolk, IP14 3BW
E-mail: info@kevinmayhewltd.com

© 2003 David Gatward

9 8 7 6 5 4 3 2 1 0

ISBN 1 84417 047 0
Catalogue No. 1500578

Cover design by Jonathan Stroulger
Edited and typeset by Elisabeth Bates
Printed and bound in Great Britain

Contents

Introduction

Monday mornings, especially those after a break from work, fill everyone with dread. For some reason, as the alarm wakes you up, the bed feels the most comfortable it's ever felt. You want to stay in it for ever. You try to convince yourself that you're ill, that you've a migraine, that the car's broken down, that you're snowed in. But to no avail. So you get up, bang your toes on the legs of the bed, then on the door, and finally on the toilet. You look at yourself in the mirror and pray to God that you really don't look that bad. A few minutes of scrubbing and shaving and washing and scraping doesn't seem to make much difference. It seems that the face staring back at you, the one that only days before was happy and relaxed and full of life, really is the one you have to take with you to work that day. So better just get into those clothes and have some breakfast. But the phone rings, the toast is cold, the car's got a flat tyre, and then the traffic is utterly horrendous. And as you look into the driver's mirror and see someone in the car behind thinking the same as you, you realise that this is just another day in just another life.

Or is it?

Take a look at your life again and start with this: just how lucky are you that you are alive? Well? Just for a moment try to imagine not being, to have never existed, to have never been given the chance to experience this world. Now think what you can do with your life, what you're capable of, what possibilities there are for you.

Think further, think of all the people you know, your relationships with them, what you've been through together, the things you've learned, the things you've done, how you can help each other discover more about what you're capable of. Is your perspective changing?

We all have those days which seem like just another day. And we all experience that feeling that we're nothing more than just another life in a billion other lives. Well, in some ways it's probably true, but in many ways it isn't. The trick is to make sure that nothing of what we've got is ever wasted. And if it is, if everything is so awful that we feel like simply giving up and fading away, we get back up off the floor, brush the dust off our knees, and get living again.

Believing in God, having faith, trusting, can be very difficult when the days fade into weeks, months, years. It's hard to think there's anything more to life when all it seems to do is just drag on from one morning to the next, enabling you to do nothing more than try to pay the bills, wishing you'd managed to get yourself a better career, no matter what it is that you do. And it's at points like this that we forget what having God in our lives really means. Jesus proved one thing above all, and that is that God wants to get involved, wants to get his hands dirty, wants to know us. What we forget is that we have to do something to help make this happen. We can't just sit here expecting God to be a part of our lives, in just the same way that we can't expect friendships to work if we don't get on the phone, write letters, visit. Relationships are, after all, a two-way thing. And if that's the case, then God's desperate to be a part of our everyday lives. He wants to hear how we feel when we wake to another rainy day with no milk in the fridge. He wants to be with us as the photocopier breaks down yet again. He wants to help us stay awake as we sip another coffee trying to meet a deadline that probably, in the grand scheme of things, isn't really that important at all. This is a God who wants to help us and love us and feed us and be with us. We are everyday people with everyday lives, but what we need to do is remember that it's our everyday God who'll help us turn it all into a life worth living.

Monday mornings

How can it possibly be
   a quarter to seven?
If feels like I only went to bed a few minutes ago.
But here I am,
   sleep making my eyes
   feel like a well-gritted road
   as I try to find a reason to stay in bed.
But there isn't one.
I'm not ill,
   I haven't got a blinding migraine,
   I'm not snowed in,
   and the office hasn't been miraculously obliterated.

Looks like a cold morning out there.
Hardly something I want to experience.
This bed's much cosier,
   much more comfy.
Why can't I just work from here?
What's wrong with that?

There goes the alarm again.
It's a bit like being reminded to get out of bed
   by an insane drill.
Why, after all the years,
   it hasn't got any easier to get up in the morning
   I'll never know,
   but Mondays always seem to be worse.
Especially after a holiday.

A holiday that soon becomes memories, photos,
    and really bad souvenirs.

Right, sit up . . .
    stretch . . .
This is it.
It's time to face this one single day,
    these 24 hours of my life
    that I know I'll be wishing away.
I know it's just another day,
    but that's what annoys me.
I don't want it to be.
I don't want to waste my life
    wishing for weekends or weeks
    in the sun.
These days have got to count for something,
    anything.

Lord,
    as I face this morning,
    help me to make sure
    that it really isn't
    just another day
    in just another life,
    but something that counts,
    that matters,
    that has purpose.

Be with me today,
    and everyday, Lord.

Amen.

Bruised toes

Ouch!
How is it possible
   that something so small
   can hurt so much?
I mean, it's not like I don't know
   where my toes are.
I've had them for years.
They're at the end of my feet
   which are neatly at the end of my legs.
And it's not like I'm growing so rapidly
   that each morning my toes
   are further away.
I haven't done any actual growing for years,
   except perhaps outwards.

Look at it,
   it's bleeding now.
What a way to start the day.
I bet it's going to bruise as well.
I wonder if it's broken?
That'd be a bonus.
I'd have to go to the doctor's,
   get it checked,
   perhaps have a bandage.
I wouldn't be able to drive.
A week off work, perhaps?

Try standing . . .

Well, it was an empty hope I guess.
A few minutes of jumping around
   like a crazed flamingo,
   a bit of blood,
   and that's it.
Not a broken bone in sight.
What a waste of a stubbed toe.
Why couldn't I have tripped as well?
Fallen onto the edge of the bed?
Twisted my knee?
Been knocked unconscious?
Broken my leg?
There's no justice on a Monday morning.

Time to put on those working clothes.
And to think that years ago
   I swore never to wear stuff like this.
A grey man?
Me?
Mr Not Noticeable?
Well, so it seems now.
Now that I have deadlines,
   bills,
   a mortgage.

Well, my toe doesn't hurt any more.
Looks like the odds of me having to go to work
   are increasing.
Better get on with it I suppose.

Lord,
   as I stand here in my working clothes,

as my toe gradually stops throbbing
and my body shouts at me for a mug of coffee,
give me just an ounce of courage.
The world of deadlines and debts
    scares me,
    but I can't run away.
I'm a part of it,
    and it's a part of me.
What I have to do is make sure that despite it
    I can make something of these wakeful hours
    and arrive home knowing that those hours
    haven't been wasted.

Amen.

Toothpaste and coffee

Why do I always insist on getting dressed first,
   before brushing my teeth?
What is wrong with me?
Now I've got the faint smudge of toothpaste
   down my shirt,
   and my coffee tastes just a little bit . . .
   . . . minty.

Everything in the morning
   always seems to be a case of rushing.
Rushing to put your clothes on,
   rushing to make breakfast,
   rushing to check the post,
   rushing to defrost the meat for tea.
It can't be healthy.
And before I know it,
   I'm rushing into my car
   to rush to work.

My timing doesn't seem to be all that good.
It's not like any of this stuff takes all that long.
If I just got out of bed in time
   I'd probably be all right.
But instead,
   I ignore the insane alarm clock
   for as long as possible,
   take far too long getting out from under the warm duvet,
   and then all the other stuff I have to do
   gets crammed into a few minutes.

This isn't a healthy way to live,
   but I've done it like this for so long
   that it's hard to break the routine.
And sometimes it's the routine that keeps me going.
But then sometimes it's the routine
   that makes me want to grasp hold of my life
   and chuck it out of the window.

And now my toast has gone cold
   and once again I haven't walked the dogs
   or sorted out what's for tea.
Hard to believe I used to look forward to being grown-up,
   to being older,
   having a career,
   a house.
Now I hanker after the days when all I had to worry about
   was which essay to write,
   which pub to go to.

Lord,
   I'm scared that what I am now
   is how I'll always be.
I'm frightened that what I'm now doing with my life,
   is all I'll ever do.
That this is it.
That there's nothing left to get excited about,
   nothing left to achieve.
But that can't be right.
If I'm to believe anything,
   it has to be that my life has purpose,
   that it's worth the living.

Which is why, Lord,
    as I munch on this cold piece of toast,
    and sip this coffee,
    I ask you to help me have courage
    and faith
    in myself,
    my abilities,
    my life.

Help me live it to the full, Lord,
    no matter how rushed my morning may be.

Amen.

More bills

Typical.
The postie never arrives before I head off for work
    unless all that needs to be delivered to my door
    is a handful of bills.

Look at it.
A pile of letters all saying in their own individual way,
    'Give me money now or else.'
This is not a good way to start the day,
    never mind the week.
I've only just been paid,
    and here I am a few moments away
    from waving goodbye to most of it.

It's at times like this
    that I wonder what the point of it all really is.
I go to work
    to earn money
    to buy stuff
    that eventually needs replacing with stuff
    I can only buy
    if I go to work
    to earn money . . .
What an idiotic circle.

Sometimes I dream of living *The Good Life.*
Carving out my own version of the TV show.
Living off the land,
    having a few animals,

saying goodbye to all the pressures of living as I do.
But idealism is exactly what it says it is -
   it's a nice dream,
   but in reality?
Not a chance.

What are the odds of me
   successfully growing veg?
And there's no way the garden's big enough
   to house a goat
   or a few pigs.
And what the neighbours would say . . .

Lord,
   I sometimes feel that the balance of my life
   is just a little bit wrong.
Then the only way I see of solving it
   is to make the balance
   shift the other way.
It seems that the only way
   for everything to be right
   is to change everything at once.
But it doesn't work like that.

I need to stop making excuses
   for not doing anything
   because it all seems so difficult.
Instead,
   what I need to do is make small changes.
I need to sort out my priorities,
   work out what I can change,
   and get on with it.

Lord,
    help me to see the big difference
    that small changes can make.

Amen.

The car won't start

Stupid car.
Stupid, stupid car.
  It's just been serviced,
  and judging by the cost
  it had the entire engine replaced,
  and now it's sitting here
  refusing to start.

I hate mornings.
I hate having to go to work.
And I hate this car.

I wonder what it was like when cars weren't around,
  when it was horse and cart.
Did people find their animals refusing to get moving?
Were they late to work because of a cart-jam?
Perhaps I could replace the car with a horse.
All I need is a field,
  lots of money,
  and a massive amount of time.
Perhaps not the best solution.

Try again . . .
Come on . . .
Please . . .

Right, I'm getting out of the car,
  going back into the house,
  and then coming out again,

pretending this has never happened.
It's sure to start then . . .

Nope.
I was wrong.
I can't believe that I'm going to have to call a mechanic.
What a waste of time.
What a waste of money.
And I need to get to work.
There's so much I've got to do!
Why won't the daft thing just sta-

Oh. It's started.
And I was so close to a day off from work.
So close and now not close at all.
Typical.

Lord,
    it seems that no matter what happens,
    I'm never happy.
I'm annoyed if the car doesn't start
    and annoyed if it does.
Where's the sense in that?
All that happens is that I end up getting stressed
    before the day's even had a chance to wake up.
It's easy to say, 'Take it easy,'
    but not so easy to do;
    to sit back,
    to deal with things as they happen
    rather than shouting at them
    or hoping they'll just go away.
Now I'm all stressed,
    and for what?

Lord,
   help me to make sure
   that when I splutter into life in the morning,
   I don't end up blowing a gasket
   or bursting a pipe.
I need to learn to warm-up first,
   to ease myself into the day ahead.

Keep me ticking over, Lord.

Amen.

Service station headlines

Look at that.
A display stand dedicated only to bad news,
   international disaster,
   and semi-nude, impossibly proportioned women.
What a way to start the day.
All I wanted was to top up the petrol tank
   and now I'm trying to deal with famine,
   murder,
   war,
   and sex.
That can't be healthy before nine o'clock.

Perhaps there should be a new law
   about morning news?
Perhaps the only news we should get
   before we really start the day
   is good news?
News that makes us want to get out of bed!
News that makes us happy no matter what the weather!
News that puts a smile on our face
   and a spring in our step!

But no one's interested in good news.
No one wants to read about the great things going on
   in the world.
It's a little bizarre, really,

that we're more interested in death and destruction
than life and creation.
That we'd rather read about something awful,
    something diabolical,
    than something awe-inspiring,
    something beautiful.

Perhaps we're just lazy.
Perhaps we're just stupid.
Or perhaps there is no reason at all.
It's just the way of the world.
But is it?
Am I to believe before I head off to work
    that nothing good is happening anywhere?
That there aren't people out there doing amazing things,
    achieving the unachievable,
    pushing the boundaries?

Lord,
    morning news seems like any other news.
Always bad,
    always depressing.
It makes you wonder what the point of life really is,
    especially as you get back into your car
    to drive to work to do a job
    you perhaps don't believe in any more.

But if I'm to have faith,
    if I'm to really believe in what this is all about,
    then there has to be more.
More to what's going on in the world
    and more to what I can do to make a difference.

Perhaps this morning is different?
Perhaps this morning I can decide
   to start changing things?
Is there something you want me to do, Lord?

Help me find my own place
   in the world's good news, Lord.

Amen.

Tractors and trailers

That's it,
  I'm writing to my MP.
A new law is needed urgently.
A law which states that no tractors,
  slow-moving wagons,
  Sunday drivers
  or cyclists
  should be allowed on the roads of this land
  until after 9am.

Don't they know I've got to get to work?
Don't they know that all the other people in this queue
  need to as well?
What are they thinking?
Why couldn't they just have waited until later?
And why didn't they pull in at that lay-by
  to let us all pass?
Some people are so selfish!

Listen to me, Lord.
I'm getting all stressed
  and for what?
Where's it going to get me?
I'm not going to arrive at work any sooner
  by shouting in my car
  at someone who can't hear me.
I'm not going to make my life better
  by getting all worked up.
The opposite is true.

I now feel angry,
   annoyed,
   upset,
   cross,
   stressed,
   frustrated.
All I've achieved is to make my head hurt a bit.

I'm sorry, Lord.
I shouldn't let these things get to me.
I promise myself I won't,
   that I won't be like so many others,
   but here I am
   doing just that.

Right, ease back on the accelerator,
   stop trying to overtake at every opportunity,
   and no more unnecessary and politically incorrect
   hand gestures.
All that's important is that I arrive in one piece,
   and hopefully sane.

Keep me safe, Lord,
   in all of life's roads.

Amen.

Roadworks without the work

That's the third set of roadworks this morning
   and not one has had any sign of work
   being done by anyone.
In fact, the second one was nothing more
   than traffic lights,
   some cones,
   and a piece of road that hadn't been touched
   by pick or shovel
   for what looked like years.

What a waste of my time.
There's no way I'm going to be at work in time now.
No way at all.
If it hadn't been for all that waiting
I'd have made it.
Just.

Do you hear this all the time, Lord?
The rantings of angry drivers?
Sorry to add to the throng.
I guess I shouldn't get too annoyed.
After all, if I bothered to get up in time
   then there wouldn't be a problem
   and I wouldn't be rushing.

I guess this is just anger at myself,
   at my own disorganisation,

my own inability to sort my life out.
It worries me that perhaps I´ll always be like this.
I get concerned that increasingly
   the things that bother me
   aren´t actually worth worrying about at all.
I seem to waste so much of my time
   getting irritated with things
   that are beyond my control,
   that in the grand scheme of things
   won´t make that much difference.

I know for a fact that
   there is more to life than this.
That my real concerns
   make this small blip
   nothing more than a storm in a teacup.
But sometimes storms in teacups
   are easier to think about
   than the real issues of the day,
   the real things in my life that I should be
   getting annoyed about
   and solving.

I know, Lord,
   that there are roadworks in my life.
I´ve set up little sets of warning lights
   around certain incidents
   so that I can avoid them at all costs.
But what I really need to do,
   is to get the work done
   and repair the damage that´s there.

Help me, Lord,
    as I sit at these traffic lights,
    to get to work on the cracks in the only road
    I should be worrying about,
    the road of my life.

Amen.

Ten past nine

I'm late.
I knew I would be,
   I just knew it.
It's only ten minutes,
   but it may as well be ten hours.
In I'll walk and everyone will notice.
It'll be jotted down,
   a black mark to add to all the others.

If only
   I'd got up in time.
If only
   I hadn't stubbed my toe.
If only
   I hadn't got caught behind that tractor.
If only
   those traffic lights hadn't been there.
If only . . .

If only . . .
I fill my life with them
   and this one, like all the rest,
   really doesn't matter that much.
What's ten minutes, after all?
All it takes is an apology,
   a bit of honesty,
   and it's all sorted.
There's more to life
   than worrying about being a bit late.

Right,
    there's my desk,
    there's the boss . . .

Lord,
    help me to make something of today,
    even if it is only to say sorry.

Amen.

Sifting through the e-mails

Who are these people?
What are they talking about?
What on earth does all this mean?
I've not been away that long,
    so how can I possibly have over 200 e-mails
    to sort through?
What on earth do they all mean?

Then there's my in-tray.
And what an in-tray it's turned out to be.
Just look at all those letters,
    files,
    notes,
    faxes . . .
My life seems to be nothing more
    than sifting through information
    other people send me
    so that I can then send it on to someone else.
How well I have done.

Right, start at the beginning.
Delete . . .
Delete . . .
Delete . . .
Is there anything more annoying
    than e-mails sent to everyone in the office
    about leaving coffee mugs on the sink?

Don't people realise I've got more important things to do?
Delete . . .
Forward . . .
Respond . . .
Delete . . .

What's this one?
What report?
Great, I'm back less than 20 minutes
    and already a piece of work is late.
Why can't I be more organised?

Lord,
    are you watching this?
Sorry I seem so angry this morning,
    it's just that everything seems to be going wrong.
And now I've been reminded
    of something I should've done
        days ago.
My fault,
    and there's nothing I can do about it.

Does my life seem rather confused?
It certainly feels like it.
Just when I feel that I'm getting a hold of it,
    it explodes and I have to start
    picking up the pieces again.
I'm not saying I want a safe life
    or a dull life,
        just one that I have some sense of control over.
Does that make sense?

Right, Lord,
   that's the e-mails sorted.
Now to the in-box.
Help me make sure
   I don't throw out anything important.

Amen.

Forgotten deadlines

Are deadlines designed to be forgotten?
Are they put in place
    simply so that we drop them
    straight out of our brains,
    on to the carpet,
    to be swept out with the rubbish?

My life seems to be dominated
    by those things I need to get done by this time
    and those things I should´ve got done by that time.
No matter what I do
    I´m chasing my tail,
    running around in circles.
It´s a race I can´t win
    and a race I can´t get out of,
    and I´m beginning to feel a little bit tired.

There are deadlines I forget
    and deadlines I avoid.
Deadlines I don´t make
    and deadlines I should make
    but don´t.
And as for the deadlines I achieved?
I´m beginning to wonder if I ever have.

Lord,
    I have this feeling that I´m the most disorganised
    of your followers.
That I´m one of the few

who are always trying to get something done
but never quite doing so.
Is that how it looks from where you are?
Am I really this useless?

I don't know, Lord.
Perhaps I'm worrying too much again.
Perhaps I'm making a mountain out of a molehill.
It wouldn't be the first time.
After all, if I think hard enough,
    there are things that I've achieved,
    things that I've done,
    deadlines I've met.
Some of them have even been really important,
    which at this moment I find hard to believe.

It seems, Lord,
    that I find it very easy
    to focus on what I haven't done
    rather than what I have.
I seem to relish the bad that's in my life,
    rather than the good.
At times I can hardly begin to imagine that my life
    is something to be proud of.
Much easier to accept it's not,
    and sit sulking.

Lord,
    I don't want to sit here
    wallowing in what I haven't done.
I don't want to sit here
    dwelling on what I should've done.

It's not getting me anywhere,
    it's not making me feel very happy,
    and it's not helping me get done
    what I've got to do today.

Help me, Lord,
    to kick myself into gear,
    and to start concentrating on what I can do,
    rather than what I've missed.

Amen.

Work colleagues

There's nothing I can do about it.
I've tried and tried and tried,
   but there just isn't any way
   I'll ever find
   novelty ties
   amusing.

They're not funny.
They don't make anyone look cool.
They're in no way stylish.
And they're certainly not wacky, wild, and crazy.

I tried one once.
Along with some mildly amusing socks
   and 'really funny' cuff links.
The experience didn't change my opinion.

That's the thing with work.
I spend a great deal of time,
   many, many hours of my life,
   working with people who in normal circumstances
   I'd never associate with.

Work seems to accentuate people's differences,
   which I guess is why the novelty tie thing came about.
I have to work with people I just don't like
   and I know for a fact
   don't like me.
I have to meet with them,

talk with them,
work with them.
And now here I am
   five minutes away from just that situation –
   a meeting with someone
   in another department
   with whom I don't see eye to eye.

Lord,
   did you ever feel like this?
Were there people you just didn't like?
I sit here wondering if that's the kind of question
   I should really be asking,
   but it does cross my mind now and again,
   especially at moments like this.

Right, this is it.
Put on the grin,
   put away the cheap jibes,
   and off I go.
Help me see the good in everyone, Lord,
   and help me to show them the good in me.

Amen.

Coffee break

I´m not addicted to caffeine.
I´m not.
I know it.
I don´t drink enough of it to be addicted.
I just like the taste.
And I just need this drink right now.

How can anyone call this coffee?
How can it be possible that I´m sitting here drinking it,
   trying to convince myself that it is coffee?
Still, it´s a break from the desk,
   from the phone,
   and the rapid-fire e-mails.

I´m tired
   and it´s not even lunchtime.
I´m weary
   and I´ve not even started
   on the work I really need to do.
I´m already thinking about
   the journey home,
   tea,
   resting in a comfy chair,
   bed.

Perhaps I can stay here for a bit longer than usual?
Will anyone notice my absence?
Probably not.
Just get a top-up . . .

You there, Lord?
I need more than liquid refreshment today.
I'm feeling mentally exhausted,
  physically tired,
  and in need of peace.
My mind seems to be whizzing all over the place.
There are so many things on my mind
  that I don't know which to do first.
There are things at work,
  things at home,
  and everything's stamped 'urgent'.
But I can't get it all done at once.

I feel like I'm about to burst,
  like my brain is bubbling and boiling.
I want to stop,
  but I can't.
I want to relax,
  but I don't know how.
I want to pray,
  but I can't find the words.

Which is why, Lord,
  over this coffee,
  I pray that my unuttered prayers,
  will be heard above the din of my life.

Amen.

Meetings, meetings, meetings

Well, that was fun.
A meeting in which everyone decided,
    once the meeting was coming to an end,
    that what was really needed
    was to have another meeting
    to sort out all the stuff
    this meeting
    hadn´t actually sorted out at all.

I can´t believe I´ve just spent a whole hour
    discussing stuff I´m not really interested in,
    that wasn´t sorted out,
    that needs discussing again
    to get sorted out.
What a wild and crazy life I lead.

I can´t believe that when I was younger
    I thought I´d lead an exciting life
    full of adventure
    and travel.
Why, then, have I ended up here?
Have I simply spent years making wrong decisions?
What´s happened?

That´s the trouble with looking back.
I find myself thinking, ´What I should´ve done is . . .´
    or, ´Why didn´t I do that?´

In reality,
    what I actually did
    was, nine times out of ten,
    the right decision at the time.

Sometimes I feel as though life
    is a bit like playing poker.
You win some hands,
    you lose others,
    and you're never sure
    who's bluffing who
    or how big the pot could eventually be.

In some ways
    that makes it more exciting,
    except for right now
    when it seems that life's got bored with playing
    and given up.

My dreams of adventure
    have been replaced
    with meetings
    about meetings
    during which people decide
    to have another meeting.
The 'fizz' I thought I had in my life
    seems to have gone
    and everything feels just a little bit flat.

Lord,
    it's my faith in you,
    your teaching,

that gives me the hope that soon
all of this will make sense.
Just make it very soon, Lord, OK?

Amen.

What, no sandwiches?

I can't believe it!
Disaster of disasters!
I left my sandwiches at home!
It's lunchtime
 and now my valuable half-hour break
 is going to be spent in a queue in a supermarket
 buying something that I could've made myself
 for about ten pence.

What a waste of time.
What a waste of money.
Still, it's a good excuse to stretch my legs.

There's one thing I've noticed -
 that sitting at a desk day after day
 really doesn't do your physique any good at all.
In the morning I don't look too bad,
 but by the evening,
 after a day of sitting in one place,
 everything seems to have gone a little bit
 pear-shaped.

What's happened to my youthful figure?
Oh, right, yeah . . . I got older.
But that's not a good excuse.
A more accurate description would be
 I got older
 and lazier.
But then I don't have as much time to keep fit as I used to.

There are so many other things I need to do.
So many other things that I have to get done,
    to fit into my already hectic day.
I've got other priorities now,
    ones I never had before.

Lord,
I seem to have forgotten about myself.
I've been so busy lately
    that other things have been pushed to the side.
I forget to have breakfast,
    lunch gets taken over by other work,
    tea is rushed,
    and fitness?
Well, I do try to run up the stairs now and again.

I feel unfit, Lord,
    and I don't like it.
It may have taken me sometime to realise it,
    but I know I need to do something about it.
Perhaps this little walk is the start of something new?
Who knows,
    before too long I may even start running again,
    and apparently there's a swimming pool nearby.

Help me treat my body like a temple, Lord,
    rather than a road-side café.

Amen.

But at the end of the day,
    it's all so uncertain.

I can have my ideas
    about what I'd like to happen in my life,
    what I'd like to experience,
    to do,
    to achieve.
Some of it's possible,
    some of it's just me with my head in the clouds,
    but all of it I bring to you.
And why?
Simple . . .
None of it is worth even attempting,
    if I don't do it with total trust in you.

Be with me, Lord,
    today,
    tomorrow,
    and for the rest of my life.

Amen.

Rain on the window

It's raining.
Again.
Absolutely tipping it down.
At least I'm inside and safe from getting drenched.

It looks horrible out there.
People running for cover,
   cars driving through rivers
   rather than roads.
Wet,
   cold,
   grey,
   uninviting.

Sounds like how I feel inside.
Like there's a wet and dreary day
   hanging around in my head.
I keep trying to escape it,
   to get out of the rain,
   but somehow it follows me,
   that little grey cloud.

I don't know where it's come from, really.
It's not like everything's terrible,
   or horrible, or rubbish.
There are lots happening in my life.
I'm busy, doing OK.
But there it is,
   floating around and making me feel low.

Lord,
   at times like this
   it's difficult to snap out of it,
   to get it together and just be myself.
Small things, small worries,
   soon become big things, big worries.
Then I start to think and worry about other things,
   stuff that just isn't important.

I know worrying doesn't help
   and I know that being low
   doesn't make things any better,
   but here I am,
   looking out at the rain
   and feeling just like a cold wet day myself.

I need to get it together, Lord,
   to pull myself round,
   concentrate on the good,
   the exciting,
   the amazing in my life.
I don't want to waste my time
   feeling like this.
It's not healthy.
All it does is make me feel worse.

Lord,
   walk with me in the rain,
   and help me find shelter.

Amen.

Is this all there is?

There's got to be more to life than this!
There's just got to be!
How is it possible that I'm here
    doing what I'm doing?
It's all so pointless,
    so worthless.

Look at me!
I'm sitting here,
    in the middle of valuable years of my life,
    and what am I doing with them?
Am I discovering?
Am I adventuring?
Am I squeezing every ounce of life
    from every minute of the day?
No!
I'm not!
I'm just wasting it
    so that I can cover some bills,
    pay off a bit of the mortgage,
    buy some food.
What is the point?

I wonder sometimes how I got here,
    what decisions I took
    that meant I should be punished like this.
It seems unfair,
    wrong,
    totally against what I've always wanted my life
    to be about.

How can I count for anything
　　sitting here doing this?
How can I ever be proud of what I'm achieving?
How can I look at my life and think,
　　´Yes, this is me,
　　this is why I'm here!
　　Look, Lord! Look!´

Lord,
　　I don't like to feel that I'm wasting what I've got.
My life,
　　my gifts,
　　my abilities.
Every day I live,
　　I'll never live again.
That's it,
　　end of story.
And when I look at the days I'm living
　　I can't help but feel that they're days
　　I could've lived
　　so much better.

But what can I do about it?
I have to get the job done,
　　do what I'm employed to do.
But what I also need to do
　　is look at the wider picture,
　　beyond what I do day to day.
I need to see my life as something huge,
　　something vast.
It's not just about today,
　　or what I do over the next couple of years.

It's about what I do through it all,
   what I achieve in its entirety.

I'm scared my life will come to nothing, Lord.
Give me courage to see my life through your eyes,
   to see what I am capable of,
   both in the small moments of my life
   and in my life as a whole.
Help me make my whole life
   something that counts,
   no matter what today may hold.

Amen.

Photocopier blues

Well, this is worthwhile.
Standing here
    with a handful of papers to copy
    and the machine's jammed already.
I've managed only eleven sheets of paper
    and now I've got to wait for the engineer.
What a complete and total waste of time.

You'd think by now that photocopiers
    would work,
    that photocopying –
    their one and only task –
    would be something they could do with ease.
But obviously not.
Photocopying, it seems,
    is something photocopiers
    still find difficult to do.

If it wasn't built like a battle cruiser
    I'd throw it out of the window.
Instead, all I can do is wait.

Lord,
    it's at times like this
    that the utter pointlessness of my nine-to-five
    really does become apparent.
This is a job
    anyone could do,

it's just that I was unlucky enough
   to get in the way.
It's a job
   that doesn't really matter,
   doesn't really make a difference.
For example,
   take me out of the equation,
   get rid of me,
   and would it really matter?
Would everything grind to a halt?
Nope,
   I'd just be replaced
   and things would go on as normal.

It's living like a robot, Lord.
Same thing every day,
   no hope of change,
   life just drifting by.
And that's why it's so difficult
   to take it seriously.
I see other people around me really into what they do.
They love meetings and deadlines
   and are almost obsessed
   with what the business is about.
They live it,
   they breathe it.
To them, it seems that this is all there is.
And they get promotions,
   higher pay,
   better careers,
   while I stay here
   getting annoyed at this machine.

But, Lord,
    the problem is that I don't want to be like them.
I can't pretend to enjoy what I do,
    be interested in it,
    be happy about where I am.
I'm not a good liar.
To me this is not what my life is about.
There's something more to who I am,
    what I can do,
    what I can achieve.
Which is why,
    standing at this spluttering machine,
    I ask you to help me through the blues of today
    and into a brighter tomorrow.

Help me to work for you, Lord.

Amen.

Paper-clip sculptures

Forty-two paper-clips,
   a cup of coffee,
   five post-it notes,
   and fifteen minutes –
   and look what I've created.

I feel so proud,
   so impressed that I can utilise my time at work
   to create something
   so different,
   so interesting –
   so pointless.

Lord,
   help me to make sure
   that the time I have
   isn't used to create a 'me'
   that looks impressive
   and serves no purpose.

Amen.

Jobsearch

It's lunchtime,
   the boss is out,
   no one can see what I'm doing,
   and I'm glad.

I can't quite believe
   that I'm sitting here doing this,
   searching for jobs.
But there wasn't that much in the paper,
   so the Internet it is.

I've got to get out of here somehow.
It's not that the pay's awful,
   or the people are terrible.
It's just that I want more.
But what?
That's the question.
What 'more' am I looking for?

I've been stuck in the same career for ages now,
   or so it seems.
I can't afford a pay cut,
   but neither can I afford
   to let this place get me down,
   ruin me,
   see me through to retirement.

But what can I do?
What is there out there that I can do

that will push me,
challenge me,
allow me to develop?

Lord,
I know that I'm lucky to at least be employed,
but there's more to a job than that.
I feel as though I've outgrown where I am
and need something more.
But searching for new jobs isn't easy.
People are looking for something specific,
something written on a CV that says
'Yep, this is the one for the job.'

I don't know what I've got to offer,
I don't know what else I want to do.
All I do know
is that I want to take what I've got
and use it properly
in the knowledge that you're with me
all the way
and that I'm on the right track.

Amen.

More coffee

One more coffee.
It seems my day is nothing more
    than a succession of trips to and from
    the coffee machine.

Am I addicted?
Am I that desperate to stay awake?
Or is it just a way to get away
    from what I'm doing,
    to give me time to think,
    to work out where I'm going in life?

Who'd have thought it, Lord,
    that a coffee could hold so much meaning?
That a simple wander from my desk,
    across the room,
    could have me questioning my very existence?

As this coffee keeps me awake, Lord,
    keep me alert to the possibilities ahead of me
    and awake enough not to miss any of them.

Amen.

Team meeting

Lord,
   I've got another team meeting
   and I don't want to go.

I haven't prepared for it,
   I haven't done the required work,
   and there's no way on earth
   that I'm going to enjoy it.

A full two hours
   of working with people
   that I don't necessarily like.
A full two hours
   discussing lots and lots of issues
   that I'm just not interested in.
A full two hours
   that I need to survive,
   regardless of the consequences.

Lord,
   help me stay focused.

Amen.

How can it be only three o'clock?

Today really has dragged.
It seems impossible
   that there are still
   two hours to go.
Feels like I've been here for ever.

Every minute of every hour
   seems to be stuck fast in treacle.
The day is in slow motion,
   desperate to come last
   in a race I don't want to be a part of.

The daft thing is,
   I'm sitting here with work to do
   but instead of doing it in the time that's left
   I'd rather gaze out of the window,
   sort through my drawers,
   get another coffee,
   count the paper-clips on my desk,
   doodle,
   gaze into space.

There are no thoughts in my head,
   no questions.
I'm just sitting,
   sitting,
   sitting.

Lord,
    in these last two hours of the day,
    help me to make them count.
The work I'm doing
    may not be the kind of work
    that governments depend on
    or that changes the world.
It's not interesting,
    it's not going to change my life,
    it just needs to be done.

Keep me going, Lord,
    especially when I really don't want to.

Amen.

A cold evening

Well, that's it,
   another day done,
   another few quid to take home.

It's cold out here
   and the car looks frosted over.
Still, at least it's the end of the day,
   and probably the best bit of it.
Can't believe I feel that.
Can't be a good sign.
Mind you,
   I felt OK last week.
Probably just a simple case
   of office blues.
Everyone suffers from it
   now and again.

Right,
   into the car,
   start her up,
   get the radio on,
   and head home.

Home.
Now there's a place I've been dreaming of
   all day.
Seems crazy to wake up,
   scrabble to work
   only to spend the whole day

desperate to get back
to where I started from.

Is this the way it's going to be
     for ever?
For the rest of my life?
I hope not.

You listening, Lord?
You looking at me,
     hearing the questions,
     wondering like I am
     about what I'm doing,
     where I'm going,
     where I'll end up?

The thing is,
     as I sit here waiting for the car to warm up,
     I don't regret any of the decisions
     that have led me to where I am.
And that's got to be a good sign,
     hasn't it?

Lord,
     I guess I'd better set off,
     head out into the river of traffic
     that's flooding the roads between here
     and home.

Get me there safely, Lord,
     don't let me drown.

Amen.

Traffic jam

What is going on?
Look, just get out of . . .
Oh, what?
Now . . .
Come on!
Oh, please . . .
For crying out loud!
No, don't do that!
And where do you think you're going?
Hey, bud, don't push in.
What the . . .?
How long is this going to take?
Oh, and now the traffic lights have changed.
How fabulous.
Roadworks?
But where did they come from?
Someone just move, please!
Are you blind?
Look! It's a green light – move it!

JUST LET ME GET HOME!

Lord,
    my knuckles are white
    from gripping the steering wheel.
Everyone,
    including me,
    is driving annoyed,
    going nuts just trying to get home.

And the emotion,
    the frustration,
    is beginning to show in our driving.

I want to get home, Lord,
    but there's no point getting there stressed,
    annoyed,
    angry,
    in an ambulance.
This is a small journey I know,
    but help me keep my head.

Get me home, Lord,
    in one piece.

Amen.

What's for tea?

In a few minutes I'll be home.
Journey's at an end,
   the day's slowing down
   and tea-time beckons.
Marvellous.
I wonder what I'll be having?

Didn't realise I was so hungry.
But then, when are a couple of sandwiches
   and a biscuit or two for lunch
   all that filling?
I could really go a steak,
   or perhaps a Thai curry,
   maybe even some pasta.

Right,
   I'm going to get in,
   take off my coat,
   get the kettle on for a nice cup of tea,
   then open the fridge
   and bathe in the light
   as it shows me what I can eat.
Fantastic.

OK, Lord,
   here I am,
   home at last.
That's the kettle on,
   now through to the fridge and . . .

Oh.
It's empty.
Great.
Now I've got to go back out again,
  thanks to my not being organised.

Lord,
  will I ever get the little things right?
I seem to get myself so caught up
  in the big stuff in my life
  that I forget to keep the little things in check.
Silly really.
After all,
  if I can't get them right,
  what chance have I got
  with the more important things?

Well, back to the car again, Lord,
  and off to the shops.
Help me make this the first of the little things
  that I get organised
  and from then move on to the bigger things
  that really matter.

Amen.

At the supermarket

Look at all this food.
Just how lucky am I
    to be able to just walk in here,
    pick up bits of this and that,
    put it in my basket,
    and then buy it?
Very lucky, that's how.

Here I am,
    slowly browsing the isles,
    wondering what to choose,
    what to eat.
Deciding whether to buy something different,
    something a bit more exotic.
Or perhaps to treat myself
    and go for something a bit more special?

Don't let me take this for granted, Lord,
    instead help me to remember how fortunate I am
    and to never forget to say thank you
    for the life I've been given.

Amen.

Beans on toast
and bedtime

How typical.
I come home from work
    and there's nothing in the fridge.
So I take a drive out to the supermarket.
I spend an hour wandering around
    picking food from here and there,
    fill my trolley sky high.
And now,
    back at home,
    I'm so tired
    that all I can be bothered to cook myself
    is beans on toast.

Makes me wonder
    if any of what I bought
    is what I really need.
I mean,
    there's a fair amount of stuff in there
    that I could probably do without,
    and lots of other things
    that aren't really all that good for me.
But I bought them,
    and now they fill my fridge and freezer.

Lord,
    I seem to be so easily misled
    by packaging.

I find it mind-bogglingly easy
   to convince myself that I can afford
   this and that,
   or that I need this
   or the other,
   when in fact I probably don't need any of it.

What's wrong with me?
Nothing really, I guess.
I'm just a normal person
   who occasionally gets led by the stomach
   rather than the mind.

Am I being greedy, Lord?
Sometimes I wonder.
But then is there anything truly wrong
   with spoiling myself a little
   now and again?

That's it, isn't it, Lord?
Spoiling myself now and again,
   rather than every time I set foot
   inside a supermarket.
There's nothing all that wrong with a little luxury.
It's when it takes over,
   becomes the norm,
   gets taken for granted,
   that the problems start.

I don't want to be like that, Lord.
I want to be for ever grateful
   for what I have,

for what I've been given,
   for the life I lead.
I've got so much,
   my life is so full.
My everyday choices are so varied
   that sometimes I forget
   just how blessed I am
   to be in a position
   to make a decision.

Lord,
   I don't want to live a life
   where luxury is the norm.
I don't want to exist only for what's the most expensive,
   or what's the best I can get,
   regardless of the cost.
Instead,
   I want to appreciate everything around me,
   and thank you for all of it,
   each and every day of my life.

Amen.

Thank God it's Friday

Lord!
God!
It´s Friday!
Wahey!
The week´s over,
   and it´s the weekend!

No more work,
   no more pointless meetings.
No more deadlines
   and no more conversations with people
   who bore me
   senseless.

No more moody photocopiers,
   psychotic staplers,
   pens that run out,
   pencils that break,
   telephones that never stop ringing.

It´s the weekend
   and it´s time for a break,
   a rest,
   a bit of ´me´ time.
Time to live a little,
   to do some of the things I love,
   to speak to some of the people who make my life
   what it really is.

It's the weekend, Lord.
It's time to chill out a bit,
    sit back and be me,
    relax.

Make sure I don't waste it, Lord.

Amen.

Staying in, not going out

Years ago
   I´d have been out of the door like a shot.
I´d be all dressed up,
   would´ve phoned a few mates
   and we´d all be meeting up for a night out.
A night of parties and pubs.
A night of friendships and fooling around.
A night of chatter,
   music,
   laughter.

I´m older now, though.
Friday nights have changed a bit.
People have moved on,
   those years are now a memory,
   and now I quite fancy just sitting in for the night
   and doing nothing more
   than relaxing,
   letting my mind melt.

It´s weird, Lord,
   how those times that seem to last for ever
   suddenly disappear.
My memory is packed full
   of nights out,
   times with friends,
   days that made you feel immortal.

But now?
Now I'm different.

These are memories
   that I can dine out on,
   or just stay in and enjoy in my own time.
These are memories
   that have played their part
   in making me who I now am.

These are memories
   that I don't want to forget
   and at the same time
   must accept that I'll never experience again.

Sometimes that's a depressing thought.
I want to be that age again,
   mixing with the same crowd,
   doing the same things.
Life, at times,
   is difficult to accept.

Growing older, Lord,
   sometimes gets me down.
There I am, enjoying myself,
   happier than I've ever been,
   when life moves on,
   people move on,
   everything changes;
   and what is
   becomes what was,
   and is soon a memory.

Did you feel like this, Lord?
Did you ever want the moment
   to stay how it was for ever?
Did you wish that you could stop the time,
   enjoy where you were for eternity?
Was it hard to grow up,
   to become who you eventually became?

Half the problem, Lord,
   is that I'm still not completely sure
   who I am.
I've experienced so much,
   but years ago I was sure that by now
   I'd be satisfied,
   happy,
   successful.

But I'm not.
I'm still me,
   just a little bit older,
   a little bit more jaded,
   a little bit wiser.
I've done more,
   experienced more,
   seen more,
   but I'm still me.
The me back then,
   sitting here now,
   looking back and realising
   that I haven't changed all that much at all.

That's frightening, Lord.
It means that when I'm 60,

I'll still be the same old me.
That when I'm only a few years from death,
    the only real difference
    will be my body,
    its age,
    its inability to do the things
    I still take for granted.

And this is where staying in leads me, Lord.
To you,
    to thoughts about my future,
    to questions about what I'm doing,
    where I'm going.
Thinking about the answers
    and wondering if I'll ever find them,
    wondering whether,
    as I sit here and gaze into the future,
    who I am
    will ever make sense.

Help me to understand myself, Lord.

Amen.

Early night

I'm too tired to stay up any longer.
It's been a tough week
   full of deadlines
   and pressures
   and discussions.

All I want to do
   is to lie down,
   close my eyes
   and sleep.

Lord,
   watch over me.

Amen.

Saturday mornings

What am I doing?
It's Saturday morning
   and I'm getting up at 7am!
What's going on?
It's not like I'm off to work.
Seems my body clock
   is far too programmed.

Oh, well,
   may as well make the most of it.
A few extra hours of the day to enjoy.
Excellent.

Lord,
   what did you do at the weekend?
Did you ever have time off?
A break from what you were doing?
I guess you must've done.
No one can keep going and going
   without a break.

I sometimes get to thinking
   about what you did when you weren't out preaching
   and teaching
   and healing.
What did you get up to?
Where did you hang out?
What did you and your friends do to relax?

That's the odd thing about believing in you, Lord.
The idea that you were both God
   and man.
Strange.
You had that heavenly power
   and yet that earthly understanding,
   and it's that which draws me to you.
The idea that you understand what it's like
   to wake up on a morning,
   to look out and see the day before you.
That you know the feel of rain on your skin,
   have seen wind racing waves against the beach.
Or that you had close friends,
   worked with them,
   laughed with them,
   ate and drank with them.

God made human.
Awesome.

And it's in that heavenly humanity
   that I'm drawn to you, Lord.
It's in the knowledge,
   as I rise on this day,
   that you have done the same.
That you've seen the sun
   which is right now shining through my window.
That you've woken,
   got out of bed,
   stretched,
   and looked to the day ahead,
   wondering what it holds.

Meet me this Saturday morning, Lord,
  as your friend,
  your follower.

Amen.

A decent breakfast

Breakfast.
Most important meal of the day.
And boy, is this one something else!
Just look at it!

Cornflakes,
    coffee,
    bacon, eggs, and mushrooms.
Marvellous.
My mouth is watering big time!

For some reason,
    moments like this,
    moments that are so simple,
    often mean so much.
Those moments
    when everything else is forgotten
    and you're allowed to just enjoy what you're doing,
    to taste life.

It seems that I manage so often
    to fill my life
    with things that simply aren't important.
I spend so long rushing round
    or planning when to rush around
    that I forget the little things in life,
    those moments that make it all worthwhile.

Lord,
    it's in moments like this

that I really feel the essence of life.
It's when I'm doing something
   as simple as making breakfast
   that I find myself
   discovering afresh
   who and what I am.

It's in the simple moments,
   the simple times,
   that I find myself,
   and you.

Meet me in the spaces, Lord.

Amen.

A walk to the shops

What a lovely morning!
Can´t believe
   that I was thinking of having a lie-in.
I´d have missed all this.
These fresh early hours,
   the taste of the day in the air.

Now what was it I´m to get from the shops?
Where´s the -
   oh, great . . .
   I´ve left the list at home.
I´m bound to forget something now.
And I bet it´ll be the only thing on the list
   I really need to get.
Oh, well,
   never mind.

Doesn´t seem too busy today.
Perhaps that´s because I usually arrive here
   about two hours later than now.
Just how lazy am I sometimes?
Got to sort that out.

Right,
   there are the shops.
Now, what was it I needed?

Lord,
   as I walk into town today,

help me to appreciate anew
this world in which I live.
Help me to look at it through fresh eyes,
   to experience it,
   to breathe it in,
   to love it.

I want to learn something today, Lord.
I don't want to waste these moments that I have.
It's not a selfish thought,
   just one that means I don't want any hour
   that I'm alive
   to be one that just disappears,
   wasted,
   lost.

OK,
   there's the butcher's.
I've got a pretty good idea of what I want from there,
   and then I'll head off to the market down the road.
What a great day to be alive!
What a great morning!

Thank you, Lord,
   for helping me make sure
   that none of what today may hold
   is something that I'll miss.

Amen.

Saturday night TV

What am I doing?
This is total rubbish!
Every channel
   stuffed full
   with chewing gum for my brain.

It's junk-food, that's all it is!
Quick,
   easy,
   convenient,
   and put together with next to no effort.

I'm appalled that I'm sitting here
   watching it.
I'm amazed that I haven't turned it off.
I'm disgusted that I can't think of anything else to do.
What's wrong with me?

There.
It's switched off.
The room is now no longer witness
   to various examples of ways to insult
   my intelligence.
What a relief.

Now what?
What shall I do?
Well, there's a few jobs that need doing.
Or I could read,

listen to the radio,
    write a letter.
Watch a bit more telly . . .

Lord,
    it's strange how the easy option
    is so often the option I choose.
I guess at times I'm just lazy.
Other times it's because I don't think.
Then there are those days
    that just become routine.

Not very rewarding though, Lord,
    I have to admit.
Especially when I find myself looking back
    and realising that a whole week has flown by
    and from it I've learned nothing,
    experienced nothing,
    done nothing.
All I seem to have done at times like that
    is live from one day to the next
    not really thinking,
    just existing.

Not good,
    is it, Lord?
I'm sorry,
    I don't mean to waste what I've been given.
It's just that at times
    it's the easiest way to live,
    the best way of getting through,
    of surviving.

Perhaps I could start from this minute
   to make a difference?
Doesn't take much effort does it, really?
All I have to do is make a small change here,
   another change there.
Then,
   in time,
   perhaps my life will be so full
   that I'll yearn for moments to just take the easy option.
Imagine that, Lord!
A life so full,
   that laziness is a luxury!
Seems a much better way of living, Lord.

Fill me, Lord,
   with the life you know
   I have the potential
   to live.

Amen.

At church

It's quiet, Lord.
The church is surprisingly warm,
    the wind can just be heard wailing around the walls
    and there's a faint smell of candles burning
    in the air.

In some ways
    I want this moment to last for ever.
There's a sense of peace here, Lord,
    a sense of everything being still.
There's history here, Lord,
    in these walls.
I can feel it.
A sense of the people
    who've worshipped in this place,
    who've come here to kneel in your presence,
    ask for your guidance.
Of those who've come here for your protection,
    for your love,
    for your peace.

It's humbling, Lord,
    to know that these walls
    have seen so much,
    heard so many voices
    calling your name,
    speaking to you.

I'm a part of that history, Lord,
    a part of the generations of people

who have searched for you,
sought you out.
And it's in the knowledge of what has gone before me
and the thought of what is yet to come
that I sit here,
silent,
reaching out to you.

Sit by me, Lord,
in this place of saints.

Amen.

Sunday lunch

Now this is a proper meal!
The one I look forward to
   all week!
And the one, Lord,
   that I at least try to remember
   to say thank you for.

So, Lord,
   for this food
   and for my life,
   for everything I've been given
   and for everything I will come to do,
   I give you thanks.

Your generosity
   overwhelms me.
Your trust in me
   makes me humble.
Your love
   gives me purpose.

Take my life, Lord,
   as a thank-you
   for everything I have,
   everything that you have given me.

Amen.

Is it really
Monday tomorrow?

I'm so tired.
All I want to do
   is put my head down on this pillow
   and disappear
   off into the night.

It's the end of the day
   and I've got tomorrow to look forward to.
Not sure that I am though.
There's stuff I need to get done,
   stuff I didn't get done from last week
   and stuff that I know is just going to turn up
   and get in the way.

I'm not even in bed
   and I'm already thinking about tomorrow,
   worrying about it,
   wondering what I'm going to do,
   how I'm going to do it.
But worrying never changed anything.

Lord,
   it's difficult when a weekend draws to a close
   and the week stares you in the face.
It's hard to just grin and bear it.
There are pressures ahead,
   decisions.

There are things I have to do
    that I don't necessarily want to.
It's another week
    in my ordinary life
    that I so desperately want to be
    extraordinary.

I'm going to bed now, Lord.
It's time to say goodbye to Sunday
    and hello
    to Monday.
I need a good night's sleep,
    a fresh mind,
    an alert brain.
But I also need peace,
    and it's a peace I know I can only get
    through you.

Keep me calm, Lord,
    as I wake to a new morning.

Amen.